Pick a Pet!

by Lucy Floyd

Orlando   Boston   Dallas   Chicago   San Diego

Visit *The Learning Site!*

www.harcourtschool.com

Here is a store.

It's filled with pets!

The pets are fed.
They are in a pen.

The pet man can
help you.

"See the red one?"
the man said.

"I pet her every day!"

What was the pet
for you?